Unleash your 'Business' Potential

Idea-rich ways to out-market, out-think, and out-perform your competition, 'even' in tough times!

Bob 'Idea Man' Hooey

Author, Why Didn't I THINK of That?

"Go confidently in the direction of your dreams. Live the life you have imagined."
Henry David Thoreau

Brain waves, ideas, and plans…

How to gain the winning edge on your competition, 'even' in tough times

We have encountered *'tough times'* in the past and are currently working through another series of challenges on a global level. These are the times when our creativity and persistence are stretched. These are the times when our commitment to growth and profitability are challenged. These are the times when we prove to ourselves and our clients just how good we are.

There are many ideas which, when acted upon, give you a competitive edge. They will enable you to **out-market, out-think, and out-perform your competition**, even in tough times. In fact, when I sat down to think of a few for this publication, I came up with over 60 off the top of my head. And I was just warming up… ☺ Bet you can add to these!

My original *brainwave* was to encourage you to establish a weekly focus - a program of innovation and continuous improvement in your career and your business. If you stop growing, you will find yourself stagnating. The end result - being left in the dust by a competitor or colleague who is still on-the grow.

I've included a variety of ideas for your consideration as an idea-rich kick start. **I'm sure you'll find it profitable reading.**

Don't forget to take a break to recharge, refocus, and relax. Since your competition may not be as disciplined and may not be establishing systems or processes to encourage consistent growth and development, and you are – taking a few well deserved weeks off each year will work wonders. It's good for your brain, your body, and your sanity. It's a great way to reward yourself for a job well done each year.

It's also good for your business and your creative process. Your ideas will percolate even better while on vacation. At least, that's my story. ☺

I also know that once you firmly embed the process of being on the look out for creative or innovative ways to grow your business to the next level, 'even' in tough times, you'll succeed. **I want you to work 'less' and be more 'profitable', by working smarter with better systems in place.** Most of my writing, live consulting, motivational speaking and training programs are *predicated* on this belief.

Keep a continual focus on capturing or generating ideas. Then implement these new ideas, systems or processes on performance, thinking, sales, and marketing.

This will allow you to expand and unleash your 'business' potential.

Three '*key*' ways to strategically increase your business:

Increase the number of clients you attract to visit and retain to deal with you – recruitment and retention.

Increase the average size of the sale for each client – up-sell!

Increase the frequency or number of times each client returns and buys from you again – turnovers and repeat business!

To fully **Unleash Your 'Business' Potential,** you need to create a process that allows you to explore and engage each of these three areas. Each area will have its own challenges and opportunities for innovation and success. Take time weekly, to review one of my idea nudges, and see if you can apply it in your situation. Perhaps something even more innovative will come to you? Act on it to sensitize your team in helping your clients and your business succeed.

Encourage and reward innovation as a business-building tool!

Consider these tips as you **Unleash your 'business' potential:**

Apply the innovative process to your situation: Preparation; incubation; illumination; and implementation, or action on creative thoughts.

Believe in your creative abilities. ***Belief precedes creation!***

Don't be afraid to ask '*stupid*' questions. There aren't any!

Challenge your assumptions and existing mindsets.

Give your ideas breathing space to germinate and grow.

Read outside your normal zone to expand your mind.

Recruit a creative, collaborative circle of friends and fellow innovators.

Travel and be open to explore and expand by truly '*seeing*' new ideas.

Add any new ones that sprang to mind as you read through these:

"Opportunities don't happen. You create them." Chris Grosse

More idea-rich mental nudges

Learn to explore the World Wide Web. Visit us at: **www.ideaman.net**

Make a conscientious effort to capture, review, and act on your ideas.

See your **Ideas At Work!** by using the four critical building blocks: **Planning; Passion; Persistence**; and of course, **Patience**.

Remember to have fun! We learn best in times of enjoyment.

Use "Thunder-thinking" or targeted brainstorming to live outside your box.

Share and expect synchronicity with the world.

Encourage idea volume generation with all your connections.

Unleash Your 'Business' Potential is based on simple principles – of being aware and observant of opportunities to better serve your clients. Focusing your efforts on increasing your top line, in addition to keeping an eye on your bottom line. Creating a ***culture of***

innovation that includes and inspires everyone in your team as a partner in your success.

Your future leans heavily on what I call the **3P's of business success**:

Positioning: Constant effort on your part to ensure you are positioned in the minds of your clients, with the products and services they need, before they need them! A success foundation!

Promoting: Constant effort to ensure they know who you are, what you can do for them and where you are located. Business basics 101

Performing: Constant effort, by every member of your team. Ensure that each client contact is a positive one that reinforces your commitment to serve them, now and in the future. Customer Service!

Here are another trio of ideas that effectively illustrate what I mean:

Sylvan Goldman, created the first shopping cart to assist his clients in his two supermarket chains in 1937 He'd noticed his customers bought only what they could carry around the store.

Kemmons Wilson realized families found it difficult to find affordable hotels, so he opened the first Holiday Inn. He made it easier for families to enjoy their vacations and venture further across North America. He set a standard of service excellence as well.

Roy Speer and Lowell Paxson noticed people liked shopping as well as watching TV. The Home Shopping Network, a 24-hour TV shopping channel was launched. Again, being aware of trends, people's habits and routines, lead to a new distribution channel that has benefited millions of shoppers and 1000's of retailers.

With the advent and development of the Internet, our global playing field exploded with new opportunities and new competitors. There is a myriad of opportunities for *'someone'* to unleash their 'business' potential in your field.

Will you be the *'one'* to take advantage of them, and **use the power of applied innovation – Ideas At Work! to re-invent your future and your organization?**
Bob 'Idea Man' Hooey

Table of contents

How to gain the winning edge on your competition, 'even' in tough times 3

More idea-rich mental nudges 7

Table of contents 10

How to leverage *'Unleash'* 11

Understanding why people buy 16

Unleashing Your 'Business' Potential 21

Out-market, out-think, and out-perform your competition, 'even' in tough times! 24

Take advantage of 'business' opportunities 48

Thanks for reading *Unleash your 'business' potential* 52

Bob's B.E.S.T. publications 55

Copyright and license notes 57

Acknowledgements, credits, and disclaimers 60

Disclaimer 62

What they say about Bob 'Idea Man' Hooey 64

Engage Bob for your leaders and their teams 68

How to leverage *'Unleash'*

Unleash your 'business' potential contains a range of tips, techniques, and ideas to help you improve the way you recruit, train, and lead your team for shared growth and long-term success. It evolved into its present form with the inclusion of stories, ideas, and first-hand experience based on copious conversations, notes, and observations of productive fellow business leaders. It was made personal from my own experiences in leading and being on a variety of business and organizational teams across North America and the globe.

It has been updated (2016) with a focus to assist committed professionals and business leaders to share a few ideas. I want to help them better leverage their time to strategically invest in the lives and careers of those they lead while they enhance their careers and companies.

This is <u>not</u> just a book for casual reading. It is a book to be 'chewed', to be dipped into, and leveraged as a resource or reference guide. It is a 'work-book' with homework; and, I hope, provocative questions that help you decide what you want to accomplish with your life, your leadership, and your relationships. It is your resource, so mark it, highlight it, and make notes in the margins.

To get the best from this book, first visit the Table of Contents to identify which chapters and/or topics meet your most critical, time sensitive needs. Read them carefully and make sure you understand the guidelines and advice given. Some of the topics may not be of direct interest to you (now) depending on your needs. You may wish to read some of the other chapters so that you can understand the needs of other leaders or scenarios.

Unleash does not contain ALL the answers. It is a collection of thoughts, notes, clippings, tips, techniques, lessons learned, and ideas shared primarily from one learner, one business leader's viewpoint, mine.
It is simply intended as an aid to your reflection, learning, and inspiration – a resource that you can draw upon in preparation for your personal leadership endeavors. Its aim is to give you a creative resource that, when applied and practiced with real teams, will help you develop and build both your confidence and competence as a leader.

A more productive approach would be to take the tips and concepts presented here and blend them with your own leadership style, personality, and creativity. Keep in mind your own time constraints and 'comfort zone as a leader, business manager, or professional', to generate unique and personalized ideas on how you can create, give, and improve your interaction and action with your teams.

Unleash is designed to offer you flexibility in how you leverage it for your personal and professional use.

You can sit down for an hour or two and read it **cover to cover**. This is a great way to start by getting a feel for what is included, especially for newer or emerging business leaders who want to gain the full benefit from their investment.

A word of advice: ***Unleash*** is the result of over 29 plus years of personal study and first-hand experience in a variety of idea-rich business leadership, coaching, and support roles for executive clients and their respective teams. Once you have done a quick read of the whole book, identify particular sections or tips that interest you and work on manageable chunks.

You can select one chapter or section and work to incorporate the ideas you discover into your own leadership style and specific leadership role or personal situation. You can look at the Table of Contents and jump straight to the tips or areas of study that particularly interest you.

We have attempted to incorporate something of benefit for everyone, regardless of your current level or skill in leadership. You might even find some contradictory advice in different parts of the book! This is because there is no single, universal 'right answer' – you must find what is a right fit for you, your objective, and your team's specific needs. What works for you is what is best.

Choose it, try it, and adapt it as needed to serve you in your quest to be a more powerful and impactful leader and in taking control of how you allocate, invest, or leverage your time.

Brain boosters: (take a minute and let your brain play with one or two) Warming up your brain to engage your creative genius works!

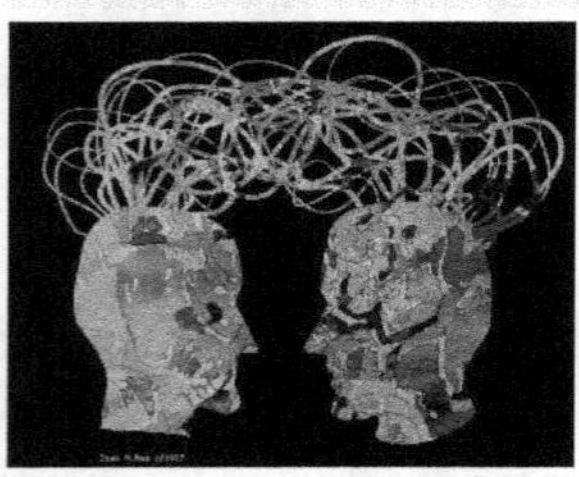

Finish this sentence 20 times: People are most generous when ___________

Design the cover for a new book called, 'The best things in life are creative'

Think of your childhood songs. Sing one to someone else today.

What if birds barked and dogs chirped? What would that be like?

Understanding why people buy

… and how I can re-position myself to take advantage of that reasoning

People make purchases, accept offers, or decide to frequent a specific store or vendor for a variety of reasons. They buy into benefits. The better you understand the reasons they buy, as related to your product or service, the better you will be equipped to convince them to buy from you. Your research and conversations with them can uncover the keys to gaining and retaining them as customers.

'Make ME Feel Special – Idea-rich customer service strategies' teaches that offering me, as your prospective client, what I really need, not just what you sell or what I ask for!

Visit: www.SuccessPublications.ca

The following benefits reflect the reasons people buy in order of importance. Remember each prospect is different, as is each product or service.

Your product or service might not offer all these benefits. That might be ok, or maybe not - you decide!

However, is there some way to modify or position your product or service to offer each benefit?

Unleash your 'Business' Potential **- offer customers more reasons to deal with you! Here are ten reasons why people make decisions to buy or engage the services of a professional or business.**

1. To make money/acquire or possess

Describe how your product or service offers me the potential for profit or a potential gain.

2. To save money or prevent future loss

Describe how your product/service offers ways to save me money.

3. To save time

Describe how your product/service can save me time.

4. For recognition

Describe how your product/service offers me recognition or status.

5. For security/peace of mind

Describe how your product/service offers me security or peace of mind.

6. For convenience/comfort

In what ways does your product/service provide for my convenience or comfort?

7. For flexibility

How does your product/service rate in flexibility? In what areas? How?

8. **For satisfaction/reliability/pleasure or entertainment**

How does your product/service stack up in these areas? Why is that important to me?

9. **For status or pride of ownership/ gratify ego or impress others**

How does your product/service add to my status or pride of ownership?

10. **For health reasons**

Is there some way that your product/service will contribute to my health?

Drop me an email and I'll send you the full list of **50 emotional reasons why people buy** something. bob@ideaman.net

Understanding the answers to these questions will give you an edge in gaining, serving, and keeping your customers. Being able to present your product or service from the perspective of meeting your client's needs, by appealing to their desired benefits, can be critical to your success.

The more you know about your client, your product/service, and your competition, the better equipped you are to effectively do business into the next century. Can you think of any other reasons why people would want to do business with you? Make a few notes here:

"Don't be afraid to give up the good to go for the great." **John D. Rockefeller**

Unleashing Your 'Business' Potential

As said earlier, when all is said and done, there are essentially three simple (although not necessarily easy) ways to increase your business.

Work to increase the number of clients you attract to visit and retain to deal with you.

Work to increase the average size of the sale for each client.

Work to increase the frequency or number of times each client returns and buys again.

If you really want to ***Unleash Your 'Business' Potential***, you need a process that allows you to work on each of these three areas. Each area will have its own challenges, opportunities, and rewards.

Look for idea-rich ways to **attract more clients** in the services and product mix you offer. Kind of like the comparison of having a single line in the water and having multiple lines with different baits. Which one will have the best chance of catching more fish? What kind of bait do you have?

How about looking for ways to add-on or cross sell?

Adding-on helps move the client to a larger or superior product, package or service. It is based on really understanding the intended use and realizing the basic product or service will fail to meet the real needs of your client.

Cross selling introduces your client to additional products or service. Offer them alternatives that perform better and are in their best interest. Phone providers like Telus does this well with bundling: Voice mail, call waiting, auto call back, 2nd line, autodial, calling cards, caller ID, 3rd line for security,4th line for fax, cable and computer information delivery systems.

Test your offerings, product mix and services offered. Experiment with your Web site, advertising, promotional materials, sales and direct mail letters, live sales presentations and in store demos, guarantees, USP's, pricing points, volume purchase and discounts, or financing. Keep refining until you find something that is effective and then update it as needed to keep it fresh and relevant to the changing market place and client needs.

Look for ways to form mutually profitable, **strategic alliances** with those companies who are already dealing with the people you would like to attract. Those companies who have already earned their trust and respect. If you offer complimentary, non-competitive services or products that assist them in serving their clients you will find a more favorable response. Look for opportunities to offer this kind of connection to people who want to deal with your clients and who offer something you don't offer or are unable to do so profitably at this moment.

Condition your mind to look for break through ideas and creative solutions. Investigate other industries, look at their success stories and best practices and see if they hold a secret that you can transfer to yours. For example: Fed-Ex simply copied the central distribution system used by the banking system at that time for courier delivery. Fred did ok with this transplanted break-through!

As my friend and fellow author Jay Abraham says, ***"Break Throughs let you out think, out leverage, out market, out sell, out impact, out defend, out maneuver, and continuously outwit your competition at every level."***

Look for **breakthrough/transferable ideas** in marketing, innovation, creative, operations, sourcing, technology, systems, process, selling, financing, product mix, service list, and distribution.

Out-market, out-think, and out-perform your competition, 'even' in tough times!

***"One can never consent to creep, when one feels an impulse to soar!"* Helen Keller**

One word as we continue: My objective here is to give you and your team a series of idea-rich '*mental nudges*'. **A reminder for getting the best value from this mini-book -** take a few minutes and read it all the way through in one sitting. This will allow you to plant a few '*idea seeds*' in your fertile mind. You might find one or two ideas that jump out at you can be '*unleashed*' immediately, or within the near future. This will allow you to start leveraging the investment you made in this mini-book - to augment the investment you continue to make in your career and organizational growth and success.

Systematically re-consider one idea-a-week. Let it '*germinate*' in your mind as you go through your week.

Does it apply to what you are doing (some may not)?

Can you adapt it and apply it immediately?

What would it take to make it feasible?

Can you see the importance of investing in making it a reality at this time?

Can you improve on it and make it even more productive?

Does it spark your creativity in bringing a new or more innovative idea to mind?

How will you implement it?
Can you track the cost savings or income potential associated with it?

When will you begin acting on it (key question)?

Enjoy the adventure!

Learn for Life! Use a portion of each day to read and expand your experience, knowledge, and awareness. The average North American reads one book a year. Investing only 15 -20 minutes daily to read, allows you to easily read 17- 20 books a year in your chosen field of study.

This will give you a real competitive advantage and increase your depth of expertise. It will also give you access to new ideas and fields, where you can apply innovation in your career or organization. **Education doesn't stop when you graduate** or when you land the job of your dreams. In sales and especially business, it is a *life-long* commitment!

You might even want to set up a reading success team, and summarize or regularly share what you read with each other.

Make more productive use of business cards – use both sides to create a mini-brochure. Some people like to use the blank sides of your card to make notes. For most of us, the '*unused*' side is a *lost* opportunity to tell a bit more of your story, your uniqueness, and your commitment to me as a prospective client. The cost to print on the back is marginal.

Create a customer focused newsletter, blog, or e-zine with tips, techniques and testimonials: Keeping in touch with your current clients, suppliers, team members, and even people in your industry is a key in marketing visibility. Let them know when something new or exciting has happened. Share your team successes with them. Outline idea-rich tips and suggestions to make their use of your products or services more effective or profitable for them.

Keep them updated on what is happening, but **don't make this an '*advertising*' piece about you.** It needs to have '***solid value***' for the reader, and a reason to want to open it and read it. Keep it simple, and value added. Give them permission to share it or send it to their friends and colleagues.

Permission to reprint *(with credits and contact information included of course)* is a great way to leverage your reach and exposure.

Look for areas of cross-promotion and joint venture opportunities with other companies or professionals: Look for new opportunities to work with other professionals and organizations. Co-op to help each other reach a larger market and to better serve your combined clients by offering a better service or expanded range of products. Look for ways to assist them in the same manner and suggest mutual benefit.

Always leave the door open. Companies change policy and suppliers. People change jobs. Situations change too. Make sure you keep your options and contacts current. Work to keep a good relationship with any potential clients – even if they say no! They might not say no at another time, or if transferred to another organization.

Make use of the new 'social' media. LinkedIn, Facebook, Twitter provide excellent opportunities to keep yourself visible.

Get and use customer testimonials in your promotional efforts. This is an amazing area where you can effectively '*leverage*' your efforts to reach new clients. When your current clients say nice things about you – ask them if they would mind sharing that in writing?

Often, they will be happy to do so. Visit: **www.ideaman.net** to see what we do with ours.

Another way to get testimonials is to do customer satisfaction surveys, or have feedback forms as a regular part of your process. I make this a part of each seminar I conduct. They help on-line and in promotion.

You'll get information that will allow you to improve your service and tools to help potential clients decide to deal with you.

For example, ***"I still get comments from people about your presentation. Only a few speakers have left an impression that lasts that long. You hit a spot with the tourism people.*** **Janet Bell, Yukon Economic Forums.** Remember, people will trust credible, third party endorsements more than anything you can tell them in your own marketing efforts.

Celebrate and reward failures. Share the lessons learned from them! Start a '*mistake'* of the month club! Encourage your team to take risks and celebrate their successes. This is a great way to reward them for succeeding. But, celebrate the failures and lessons as well. Make sure the lessons are applied and shared with the whole team. Leverage the learning and cultivate their willingness to take risks in expanding your business.

Sure, people will make mistakes – just make sure everyone learns from them!

The *'secret'* here is to reinforce the culture that empowers your team to take calculated risks in building or unleashing the potential of your business. If mistakes are shared, not hidden, the learning curve will be accelerated throughout your organization -- so will the successes!

Have fun at work – your staff will love it, and your customers will too! Take a page from some of the newer and more aggressive companies who have a culture of fun at work! This doesn't mean ignoring the basics, or the clients. It does mean more energy and a more conducive environment for innovation. People learn best in times of enjoyment. Creativity is enhanced when your brain is having fun, and you are among people who are also having fun.

Hint: People like to have fun when they do business – even if they don't always like to admit it!

Give a copy of 'Unleash' to all your clients and team members. Challenge them to innovate, not imitate! Challenge your team to come up with one *'new'* idea a week that would help them become better or more productive. Make this a part of your innovation process in expanding and unleashing your 'business' potential and you will see continuous growth.

Each idea need not be a major improvement. However, if each one nudges you ahead and makes what you do more attractive, profitable, or makes your systems more effective, you will win!

Take regular time to 'THINK', dream and plan - just as it is important for time management! I cannot stress this one enough. If you would be innovative in your career or company, and stay ahead of your competition, you must allow time for your creativity. Schedule regular time away from your '*normal*' hectic pace to dream, think and reflect on how you might be better at what you are doing. Don't force it – let it come, and write it down. This is where "MY 'Next' Million Dollar Idea Book" can come in handy. Train and encourage your staff and co-workers to do likewise! **Record and Reward!**

Write an article or column on your field of expertise. Provided you have been in your field for a while and have stayed current, you might have expertise you didn't realize. Expertise that might be of solid value to potential clients. I got started down this path of speaking and writing doing articles on kitchen design. Then by sharing ideas I had learned about business management, creativity, and customer service etc, drawn from those rich experiences. Being perceived as the '*expert*' in your field can open new doors, and draw additional '*qualified*' clients to your doorstep. Works for me, ☺.

Conduct and publish the results of a survey (do this on regular basis) to become a strategic resource to your clientele. This could be as simple as exit surveys of your own clientele. Or have someone call a decent cross section of people and ask them specific questions that might be of interest to your potential clients. Compile their answers and share the information in a special report. This could become an annual event and something that your competition cannot provide.

Use a FAQ section – frequently asked questions - to assist your clients. Systemize your business to make it easy for people to get their questions answered. If you provide an on-line FAQ section that covers some of the most frequent questions, you will make it easy for them to evaluate doing business with you. Keep it current and add questions that come along on a recurring basis.

Have a 'users' group section for your site and monitor postings (problems or opportunities.) This can be a treasure trove of information if you set it up correctly and monitor it on a frequent basis. See what people are talking about, and what secrets or tips they are sharing with each other. This can be a valued customer service function for any business, and allow you to collect data on challenges, successes, and problems for your products or services. It can even provide a strategic glimpse on new services or innovations needed to keep current or competitive in the market.

Selectively display in tradeshows (network and prospect for new business, and connect with suppliers). This can be a valuable method of getting to your potential clients, showcasing what you do or what you sell to potential buyers. It can also be a method of gathering information, feedback, and customer survey materials on your company and its product or service mix. It can also provide an opportunity to meet and recruit strategic partners and potential suppliers you would not normally meet.

Ask for additional business and referrals. Go back to existing clients. '*Farming*' referrals or additional business from your current crop of clientele is an often over-looked method to enhance the top line.

If they like you and are satisfied with what you've done to date, ask them for referrals or introductions to people they know who could benefit from your services. Make sure you have asked for, and gotten, positive feedback on their experience with you first. If that is positive, ask for the referral. Don't be afraid to come back to them with additional offers, repeat sales, new products, new services, new connections, or additional programs ***that serve their needs***. Re-selling current clients can be a very profitable use of your time and efforts.

Sponsor or co-sponsor an event (like a Sunrise Seminar, Breakfast Briefing, or a Lunch and Learn!)

Give a gift to your association, fellow business owners, staff, or your clients. Sponsor a mini-seminar that can be held before everyone heads to work – a sunrise seminar, or a lunch and learn session where people can brown bag it and hear a local expert (or me) on a topic of benefit. Provide coffee and donuts or muffins in the morning and coffee or juice for the luncheon. I've done many for organizations who are committed to seeing their leaders and teams grow.

Contact your local Canadian Association of Professional Speakers Chapter for ideas and guest speakers. Visit **www.canadianspeakers.org** for information. Tell them past National Director Bob 'Idea Man' Hooey sent you.

Create and declare a special day or holiday. Promote it widely! Hey, why not? Santa Claus was originally a creation of the Coca Cola Company. The greeting card companies designed many of our holidays, such as Easter, Mother's and Father's day. Why not have a national day in honor of something that relates to your business or the benefit you provide to your clients.

Perhaps this would be a good opportunity to partner with others to expand the reach and exposure of this event. Make sure it is either a fun event, or something of solid value in the community. Perhaps honoring a local hero or worthy cause in your community.

Delegate and train your team to free yourself up for the more productive use of your time. This important! If you are *serious* about unleashing your business potential, free up time for the more productive activities such as customer service, sales and marketing. Train your staff to cover off on the more routine stuff, so you can do what you do best.

For example, I designed a course for sales teams along these lines: ***"Creating 'TIME' to Sell!*** *– How to successfully create more face-to-face time for the sales and marketing process."*

Sponsor or co-sponsor a local award – or create your own award. Perhaps having your own special day doesn't work, but you can certainly gain exposure in this arena. Get behind a local award program as a sponsor, or better yet create or co-create your own.

For example, if you have a garden center - the best lawn or garden award, or a newspaper giving a best emerging writer award. **Be creative!**

Network outside your industry – learn and apply new lessons. Remember when they said, 'It's not what you know it is who you know?" Well, when it comes to '*unleashing*' your 'business' potential this is particularly true. The answers and innovation you seek to make your team or organization more profitable often lies in the mind of someone in a different industry.

The trick is getting to know them before this '*secret to your success*' is revealed. People outside your industry see things differently and can often shed valuable insights on your challenges. They also form a basis of mutual benefit, as advisory teams, with cross promotions, and even as a volunteer board of directors for your company. You might even set up a leadership success team from these associations.

Join your local Chamber of Commerce, networking group, or trade association. We don't succeed alone, but we can fail in isolation!

Getting out with fellow business professionals on a regular basis is good for your soul. Some of them need you and your services – but they need to know who you are first. Sharing ideas, challenges, laughs, and even a beverage or two, can work wonders in stress reduction. You then return refreshed and ready to tackle the formerly '*insurmountable*' challenges. You never know, something you hear in conversation might just be your 'Next' Million Dollar Idea! It has happened for me.

Hand written 'Thank yous'. This '*simple*' courtesy can definitely set you apart from your competition.

When was the last time you received one from someone you did business with? How did it make you feel? Did it help build a closer bond with that merchant?

This is the most effective way to show me, you appreciate my business!

Engage Bob 'Idea Man' Hooey and put his innovative, engaging Ideas At Work for your group, convention or association. Call 1-888-848-8407 (toll free – North America) to find out how you can unleash your team's 'business' potential now!

Ok, I want your business! *I would love the opportunity to explore how we might work together, and how some of my programs or consulting might be a benefit for you or your team. Visit my web sites for more information on what I bring to the table,* ***www.ideaman.net or www.BobHooey.training***

Hire a professional business coach, consultant, or mentor. Take stock of your strengths and weaknesses.

Where do you need help or a little polish to help you succeed?

Where would the services of a dedicated professional help you enhance your performance or gain additional expertise in a '*specific*' skill?

Just as professional athletes and superstars engage coaches, so should you! Select coaches or mentors that have *earned the right* to teach you and check their published expertise carefully.

Ensure you respect them and their accomplishments to facilitate a good working relationship. If you have a mentor who is investing time in you, work diligently to ensure you fulfill their faith and investment in you.

Develop and promote a company or professional web site (visit ours at www.ideaman.net and/or www.BobHooey.training). In today's global economy, if you are not easily found on the web, you are potentially dead! Your site does not need to be flashy or expansive. It does have to be professional, value-added, and accurately and attractively tell your story to potential clients.

My sites have more than paid for themselves in direct contracts from speaking, training and consulting clients, and as a tool to direct potential clients interested in hiring me. I promote them in all of my programs, my literature, my postcards, my voice mail, and my on-line articles for other websites.

I've worked to make them value-added for business owners and professionals like yourself; and for meeting planners too! They have become very valuable tools in my success!

Have your services list and catalogue on your website for ease of ordering. Direct people to visit your web site in voice mail and literature.

Make it easy for people to learn about you and your company, while you sleep. What can you up-load to make it easier for me to evaluate your service or product mix, and to do business with you? Can you use an easily updated PDF format for your catalogue?

Make it easy for your customers to search your site to find what they need and to navigate from page to page.

Turn your website into a 24/7 information and service tool. Make it resource driven and value added and they will visit, tell their friends, and come back again! This is a logical and profitable extension to your brick and mortar business and a customer service tool that levels the playing fields with the big boys in any market.

Collect client and potential client emails and publish an e-letter.

A lot has been written about this. You are throwing away money, if you are not doing this! Use permission marketing to '*farm*' names from your own clients and from people who visit your website, call your office, or deal with you. Make sure you follow CASL guidelines here in Canada. Ask them to write you on-line and use a systematic process to capture those addresses for ongoing communication and additional sales.

Use your list to share ideas, successes, staff celebrations, and to remind clients about regular services, introduce them to new ones, or send along special offers.

Become a media resource or expert in your field. Just as writing a column or article will help establish your credibility and expand your visibility, so will becoming a media expert or resource in your field. Contact your local media and let them know who you are, what your expertise covers and that you would be willing to act as a resource from time to time if the opportunity arose.

You might be surprised at the response and the coverage when they call, interview you, and share your wisdom on air, or in print. Doesn't hurt your business to be associated as a '*credible expert*' in your field.

Post card marketing to acquire new clients or keep in touch with current ones. This is an idea that has made me quite a lot of money over the past six years. I learned this idea at a conference in California. It is a very cost effective way to contact and keep in touch, because it gets past the gatekeepers to be read. People normally look at both sides of a card.

Present mini-seminars, classes, or informative talks to local community and service groups.

Draw on your expertise and experience to share your story in your community. If you need a little coaching, find a Toastmasters club and join it. That is where I got my start. It was the best investment of time I have ever made.

Letting people know what you do, and where you are, can be so easy. These local groups are looking for '*interesting*' speakers on a weekly basis. You might be surprised at how productive this method works in marketing and promoting your career or business. I got my start doing continuing education classes prior to turning professional.

Include additional offers or tips along with your invoices, receipts, packaging, and sales slips – Cross promote. This is a perfect opportunity to let your clients know about your special offers, new services, or just remind them what you bring to the table. Often clients forget about all of the products or services you offer. This is a great opportunity to share new ideas, products and services from your strategic partners with your clientele.

Remember, **"Out of sight, out of mind, out of business!"**

Of course, **they will hopefully reciprocate with their clients, so everyone wins!**

Provided their materials and services are value-added, sharing them with your clients is an ongoing commitment to their well-being – and a step to converting them into loyal fans and champions.

Look for ways to 'bundle' or sell value-added services or products. Take a tip from companies like Telus, Bell, or AT&T, which offer a special bundle of telecommunication services. What services or products can you add to make what you offer more value-added? Can you offer a *"good"*, *"better"*, *"best"* choice in your contracts or product mix? Can you cross-promote value-packs drawn from your strategic partners as well as your own services?

Build volume based reward systems – don't compete on price! One of the best ways to build your business is to entice your clients to purchase longer contracts, more products over a period of time, or to give them a reason to enter into these types of arrangements. A variation of the buy 5 – get one free, so popular with coffee shops. Tire shops use it, so do restaurants, movie houses, video rentals, hotel services, and a host of other companies. So do I in my training/coaching series! What can you build on with your clientele?

Design and promote 'product of the month' as a series of business builders. Variations on including a special offer with each invoice or receipt.

Design a promotion that rewards your clients and entices them to buy a '*special*' product or service add-on each month. Reader's Digest did pretty well with the book of the month deal, as did Columbia and other music companies in the past.

What can you do that would be broken down into a monthly instalment, series, or incentive system? For example, a wine or coffee of the month club. Hmmm, wine of the month?

Focus on the top line to grow your business. All too often we focus on the bottom line, and make changes or cuts primarily on their ability to impact this area of our business. Real growth comes from applied innovation in expanding the top line with additional sales methods, training, services, products, processes, marketing materials, technologies, systems, financing plans, distribution channels, sourcing, operations, product mixes, and service lists. These are the areas, which will develop new markets and bring in additional streams of revenue.

This will allow you to find economies of scale, build in better compensation plans, increase productivity, enhance staff training, and explore new technologies and ideas to better serve your clients. That is not to say you should ignore your bottom line – track and evaluate everything – but increase your top line to grow your business and unleash your business potential.

Teach your staff how to brainstorm and harness that power to 'unleash' your business! Take time to ensure your staff know how to creatively apply the principles of brainstorming in dealing with client challenges, problems and opportunities that crop up.

This is a business survival skill! Teaching them to look at problems as opportunities to learn, and creatively serve clients better, will make a difference in their attitude and their productivity. Create time to gather for specific brainstorming sessions to enhance your performance. This is an essential part of the innovative process.

Use bulletin boards around town as mini billboards (use every opportunity to reach me as your potential client.) This is often overlooked or considered un-professional -- Too bad! For those who see the potential to simply let their clients and potential clients know about something special this is a very cost effective method of marketing. Make sure the brochures are well laid out and professional in appearance – not slick!

They can be as simple as one page with black and white lettering on colored paper. Hire a kid to put them up, or give some to your staff members to keep with them as they travel to work. Often, they will get to places you never would. How about apartments, local stores, community bulletin boards, and other businesses in your Cross-promotion team? Great opportunities to reach new clients at a very small cost.

Cross-train your team for solid customer service and coverage. Empower your team – '*everyone*' is a customer service and satisfaction agent: In our increasingly competitive market, each team member must be able to step-up, step-in and assist a client when needed. Gone are the days and the attitudes of '*it's not my job*!"

Many companies are working with less teams and each person is now carrying more responsibility. Cross training empowers your team to take action in helping a client without making them wait for someone else. Remember to your client, each team member 'is' your company, and has an opportunity to prove you value their business!

Invest the time to train each team member to be a customer service agent and deal with client problems, concerns and complaints. Each one needs to be fully aware of your policies, guidelines, and range of services and products.

This may be one of the most productive things you can do this year!

Drive by billboards – each company vehicle can be a mobile advertisement for your business. Does your company have a delivery truck, or service vehicle? Have you fully taken advantage of turning it into a traveling billboard to tell potential clients what you do? How about putting something on the roof so those in high rise office buildings can see your website address or phone number?

How about giving team & satisfied clients bumper stickers with a catchy slogan and your URL? Or, a reverse print sign or an instant sign for their back window or bumper?

Teach to reach – hold in store training sessions for your potential clients Arrange demonstrations of services or products (in store or cross promotions.) Is there an aspect of what you do that has an '*educational,*' or '*how to*' component that can be leveraged?

For years I augmented my design business by doing kitchen design & informational seminars for potential clients. It was fun and it was very productive! And this led me into the world of professional speaking and training. www.ideaman.net

Can you apply in store demonstration style promotions seen in department stores to entice or educate potential clients about new products or services?

How about doing some as cross-promotional events with strategic partners? Of course, they will return the favor at their location!

Take time to celebrate the personal and professional successes, accomplishments, and outstanding efforts of your staff and team. A successful organization is really just a successful group of people! This can be a great morale booster for your staff or team, when they are recognized publicly for something they have accomplished. It doesn't even have to be directly related to your business – it could be something they have done in their community, or additional education accomplishments.

Several of my past employers leveraged my Toastmasters' success in their marketing efforts. This can also personalize your business. People love to know what people are doing and may decide to work with you because of a shared connection with a staff members' success. This is relationship marketing at its best!

Try crazy ideas! Time and time again, we read of what was considered a crazy idea turning into a goldmine, opening a lucrative new distribution channel, or even creating a new industry. Being creative and taking risks can be the true secret to your success. Don't let fear get in the way, but don't bet the farm on them either. A balanced approach in taking a calculated risk is the path to success.

Always give them more than they expect! This is a solid practice of good customer service, and a way to build loyalty. If you've been counting, you may have realized I have given you more than 47 Ways. Hey…I knew there were some keeners who would buy this mini-book! And, I practice what I preach.

Share your '*best*' ideas here:

Take advantage of 'business' opportunities

A profitable business is, at its very *essence,* based on innovation, solving problems, or fulfilling the real needs, wants and desires of our clients. Here's a *potpourri* sampler of how to take advantage of opportunities to expand or unleash your business potential.

Out-perform, out-think, and out-market your competition by applying some of these idea-rich '*mental nudges*'?

What business are you REALLY in? Keep asking this question, and keep adapting your business to keep it fresh. **Hint**: think in terms of customer benefits. What do your customers get when they deal with you?

What do they really want? Our updated '***Make ME Feel Special!'*** is focused on the end benefit customers get from dealing with smart business owners. Visit: **www.SuccessPublications.ca**

Transplant or adapt an idea from another industry and transform it, or adapt to suit yours and the special needs of your clients. (For example: air miles/coffee cards/buy 10 get one free deals.)

Try something that didn't work the FIRST time. It might now. With changes in technology, resources, client needs and attitudes - try again!

Use a different material or process to do a traditional job. Applied creativity and innovation count big time! Explore outside your industry.

Combine two or more products or services to create a new one. Perhaps you can work with a strategic partner to develop a new service or product that will bring mutual benefit?

Synergy works—use it!

Take advantage of the trends or harness changing interests in the market place. This is where your customer service focus and research will help, a lot! Ask questions, read outside your market and visualize applications.

Look for ways to be a value-added company or person, focusing on timely delivery of solid customer service. How can you personally make value-added changes to what you bring to your work and clients?

Profitably enhancing your career or organization is built on innovation and applied creativity. As I tell my audiences, **"Being creative is often as '*simple*' as being awake, and willing to risk by trying new or unfamiliar things and activities."** Wake up your creativity today and enhance your performance!

Applied creativity can solve your client's problems and build long-term business success.

Innovation = Ideas At Work!

Looking at your career or business from different perspectives is one secret of tapping into your inner genius. **It may also uncover or unleash your 'next' million-dollar idea!**

"Would you like me to give you a formula for success? It's quite simple, really: Double your rate of failure. You are thinking of failure as the enemy of success. But it isn't at all. You can be discouraged by failure or you can learn from it, so go ahead and make mistakes. Make all you can. Because remember that's where you will find success." Thomas J. Watson

Thanks for reading
Unleash your 'business' potential

Each time I prepare to step on the stage; each time I sit down to write or in this case to re-write, I am challenged to deliver something that will be of use-it-now value to my audience/reader.

I ask myself**, *"If I was reading this, what value would I be looking for?"***

As well as, ***"Why is this relevant to me, today?"***

These two questions help to keep me focused and clear on my objectives. They help to remind me to dig into my experiences, stories, examples, and research to provide solid information that will be of benefit and help our readers, when they apply it, succeed. That can be an exciting challenge!

I trust we have done that for you in this updated primer on more effective communication and presentation skills. ***'Unleash your business potential'*** is my attempt to capture some of the lessons learned first-hand from observing and working with some tremendously effective leaders and to share them with you.

I'd love to hear from you and read your success stories. If you would be so kind, please drop me a quick email at: **bob@ideaman.net**

Bob 'Idea Man' Hooey
2011 Spirit of CAPS recipient
www.ideaman.net
www.HaveMouthWillTravel.com

I love to keep in touch with my readers and audience members:

Connect with me on:

Facebook: www.facebook.com/bob.hooey

1-780-736-0009 Creative Office

LinkedIn:
www.linkedin.com/in/canadianideamanbobhooey

YouTube: www.youtube.com/ideamanbob

Smashwords:
www.smashwords.com/profile/view/Hooey

Follow me on Twitter: @IdeamanHooey

Snail mail: Box 10, Egremont, Alberta T0A0Z0

Brain boosters: (invest a minute to play with these)

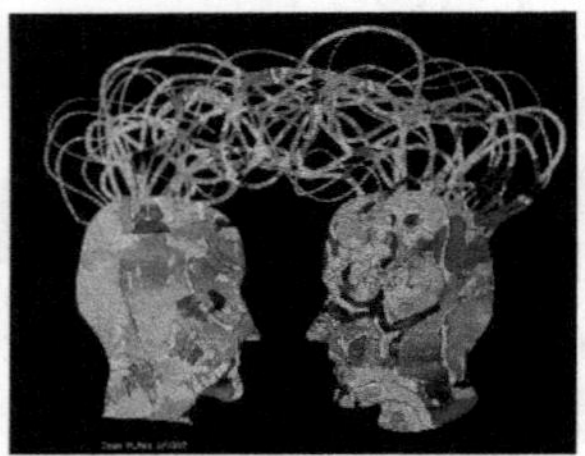

A new computer has been developed that can accurately answer any question. What three questions would you ask it?

You are a genetic engineer creating a new species of fish, using the best features of mammals. Describe your fish. Give it a name.

Bob's B.E.S.T. publications

Bob is a *prolific* best-selling author who has been capturing and sharing his wisdom and experience in printed and electronic formats for the past fifteen plus years. In addition to the following publications, he has written for consumer, corporate, trade, professional associations, and on-line publications. He has been engaged to write and assist on publications by other best-selling writers and successful companies. His publications are listed to give you an idea of the scope and topics he writes about. Bob's **B**usiness **E**nhancement **S**uccess **T**ools.

Leadership, business, and career development series *(some of them)*

Running TOO Fast (8th edition 2022)

Legacy of Leadership (6th Edition 2024)

Make ME Feel Special! Idea-rich customer service strategies (2022)

Why Didn't I 'THINK' of That? (5th edition 2022)

Speaking for Success! (10th Edition 2023)

Thinking Beyond the FIRST Sale

Get to YES! - The subtle art of persuasion in negotiation

THINK Before You Ink!

Running to Win!

Creativity Counts

Bob's Pocket Wisdom series

Pocket Wisdom for Selling Professionals

Pocket Wisdom for Speakers

Pocket Wisdom for Innovators

Pocket Wisdom for Leaders – Power of One!

Pocket Wisdom for Business Builders

Visit: www.SuccessPublications.ca for more of Bob's books.

Copyright and license notes

Unleash your 'Business' Potential – Idea-rich success strategies

Bob 'Idea Man' Hooey, Accredited Speaker, Spirit of CAPS recipient
Prolific author of 30 plus business, leadership, and career success publications

Photos of Bob: **Dov Friedman**,
www.photographybyDov.com
Cover image courtesy of **Stuart Miles** at
FreeDigitalPhotos.net
Editorial, layout and design: **Irene Gaudet**, Vitrak
Creative Services (a division of Creativity Corner Inc.,
www.vitrakcreative.com

ISBN: 978 1998014132 IS

Printed in the United States 10 9 8 7 6 5 4 3 2 1

Success Publications
a division of Creativity Corner Inc.
Box 10,
Egremont, Alberta
T0A 0Z0
www.successpublications.ca
Creative office: 1-780-736-0009

Visit our website for more information on these Idea-rich business success publications and other books by Bob 'Idea Man' Hooey.

We will be restructuring Success Publications (2022) to become more of a full publishing adventure to assist other authors in getting their messages on-line and in print. So bookmark the site and come back to see who is new.

Acknowledgements, credits, and disclaimers

As with each of my books, a very special dedication of this piece of myself, to the two people who meant the most to me, my folks **Ron and Marge Hooey**. Sadly, both my parents left this earthly realm in 1999. I still miss our time together and your encouragement and love. I was blessed with the two of you in my life.

To my inspiring wife and professional proof reader and publications coach, **Irene Gaudet**, who loves, encourages, and supports me in my quest to continue sharing my **Ideas At Work!** across the world. Thank you seems so inadequate for your timely work in helping make my writing and my client service better! I love the time we spend together!

My thanks to the many people who have encouraged me in my growth as a leader, speaker, and engaging trainer in each area of expertise including ***Unleash Your 'Business' Potential.***

To my colleagues and friends in the National Speakers Association **(NSA)**, the Canadian Association of Professional Speakers **(CAPS)**, and the Global Speakers Federation **(GSF)** who continually challenge me to strive for success and increased excellence.

To my many **Toastmasters** friends and family around the world, to whom I owe an un-payable debt of gratitude for your investment, encouragement, time, and support when I was just starting down this path; and oh, so rough around the edges.

To my great audiences, fellow leaders, students, coaching clients, and readers across the globe who share their experiences and enjoyment of my work. Your positive and supportive feedback encourages me to keep working on additional programs and success publications like this updated version. My experience with you creates the foundation for additional real-life experiences I can take from the stage to the page, the classroom to the boardroom.

My thanks to a *select* few friends for your ongoing support and 'constructive' abuse. You know who you are. ☺

Disclaimer

We have not attempted to cite all the authorities and sources consulted in the preparation of this book. To do so would require much more space than is available. The list would include departments of various governments, libraries, industrial institutions, periodicals, and many individuals. Inspiration was drawn from many sources, including other books by the author; in this updated edition of ***Unleash Your 'Business' Potential.***

This mini-book is written and designed to provide information on more effective use of your business and marketing time, as a life and leadership enhancement guide. It is sold with the 'explicit' understanding that the publisher and/or the author are **not** engaged in rendering legal, accounting, or other professional services. If legal or other expert assistance is required, the services of a competent professional in your geographic area should be sought.

It is not the purpose of this book to reprint all the information that is otherwise available. Its primary purpose is to complement, amplify, and supplement other books and reference materials already available. You are encouraged to search out and study all the available material, learn as much as possible, and tailor the information to your individual needs.

This will help to enhance your success in being a more effective business leader or professional.

Every effort has been made to make this book as complete and as accurate as possible within the scope of its focus. However, there may be mistakes, both typographical and in content or attribution. Graphics are royalty free or under license. Care has been taken to trace ownership of copyright material contained in this volume. The publisher will gladly receive information that will allow him to rectify any reference or credit line in subsequent editions. This book should be used only as a general guide and not as the ultimate source of information. Furthermore, this book contains information that is current only up to the date of publication.

The purpose of ***'Unleash Your Business Potential'*** is to educate and entertain: perhaps to inform and to inspire. It is certainly to challenge its readers to learn and apply its secrets and tips, to challenge them to enhance their skills and leverage their time to create more productive outcomes.

The author and publisher shall have **neither** liability **nor** responsibility to any person or entity with respect to any loss or damage caused, or alleged to have been caused, directly or indirectly, by the information contained in this book.

What they say about Bob 'Idea Man' Hooey

As I travel across North America, and more recently around the globe, sharing my ***Ideas At Work!,*** *I am fortunate to get feedback and comments from my audiences and colleagues. These comments come from people who have been touched, challenged, or simply enjoyed themselves in one of my sessions.*

I'd love to come and share some ideas with your organizations' leaders and their teams.

"I've known Bob for several years and follow his activities in business with interest. I originally met Bob when he spoke for a Rotary Leadership Institute and got to know him better when he came to Vladivostok, Russia to speak to our leadership. ***When you spoke I thought you were one of us because you talked about our challenges just like yours.*** *You could understand the others, which makes you a great speaker!"* **Andrey Konyushok**, *Rotary International District 2225 Governor 2012-2013, far eastern Russia*

"I still get comments from people about your presentation. ***Only a few speakers have left an impression that lasts that long.*** *You hit a spot with the tourism people."* **Janet Bell**, *Yukon Economic Forums*

"We greatly appreciate ***the energy and effort you put into researching and adapting your keynote to make it more meaningful to our member councils.*** *Early feedback from our delegates indicates that this year's convention was one of our most successful events yet, and we thank you for your contribution to this success."* **Larry Goodhope**, *Executive Director Alberta Association of Municipal Districts and Counties (retired)*

"Bob is one of those rare individuals who knows how to tackle obstacles in life to reach his dreams. He takes each as a learning experience and stretches for more. ***His compassion and genuine interest in others make him an exceptional coach."*** **Cindy Kindret,** ***Training Manager, Silk FM Radio***

"Thank you Bob; it is ***always a pleasure to see a true professional at work.*** *You have made the name 'Speaker' stand out as a truism - someone who encourages people to examine their lives and make adjustments. The personal stories you shared with your audience made such a great impression on everyone.*

The comments indicated you hit people right where it is important - in their hearts. *Each of those in your audience took away a new feeling of personal success and encouragement."* **Sherry Knight**, *Dimension Eleven Human Resources and Communications*

"Without doubt, ***I have gained immeasurable self-assurance****. Bob, your patience and your encouragement has been much appreciated.* ***I strongly recommend your course to anyone looking for self-improvement and professional development****."* **Jeannie Mura**, *Human Resources Chevron Canada*

"I am pleased to recommend Bob 'Idea Man' Hooey to any organization looking for a charismatic, confident speaker and seminar leader. I have seen Bob in action on several occasions, and he is ALWAYS on! Bob has the ability to grab his audience's attention and keep it. Quite simply, ***if Bob is involved - your program or seminar is guaranteed to succeed****."* **Maurice Laving**, *Coordinator Training and Development, London Drugs*

"I have found ***Bob's attention to detail*** *and his ability to fine tune his seminars to match the time frame and needs of the audience to be a valuable asset to our educational program."* **Patsy Schell**, *Executive Director Surrey Chamber of Commerce*

"Great seeing you in Cancun and congratulations on a job well done. ***The seminar was a great success! Your humorous and conversational style was a tremendous asset****. It is my sincere hope that we can be associated again at future seminars."* **Donald MacPherson**, *Attorney at Law, Phoenix, Arizona*

***"What a great conference**. It was a great pleasure meeting with you at the Ritz Carlton, Cancun and I shall look forward to hopefully welcoming you and your family in Dublin, Ireland someday."* **A. Paul Ryan**, *Petronva Corporation, Dublin, Ireland*

"Congratulations on the ***Spirit of CAPS Award**. You have worked long and hard on behalf of CAPS …**helped many speakers including me** and richly deserve this award. Well done my friend."* **Peter Legge, *CSP, Hof, CPAE***

"I had the pleasure of hearing and watching Bob Hooey deliver a keynote speech several years ago when he gave a presentation at a Toastmasters International Convention. ***Bob impressed me greatly with his professionalism, energy, and ability to connect with his audience while giving them value.** I heartily recommend this talented speaker and 'Idea Man' to all who want to move to the next level."* **Dr. Dilip Abayasekara, *DTM, Accredited Speaker,*** *Past Toastmasters International President*

"I attended **Speaking for Success** *in Edmonton.* ***The mark of a true leader is someone who will lay down their own pride to teach all they know to their potential successors.** To be taught by a man of his caliber was an honor whether you're a beginner like myself or a professional; the experience is well worth it! To Bob - it truly was an honor to meet you. Stay humble and enjoy the great success."* ***Samantha McLeod***

Engage Bob for your leaders and their teams

"I have been so excited working with Bob Hooey, as he has given inspiration and motivation to our leadership team members. Both at the Brick Warehouse – Alberta and here at Art Van Furniture – Michigan; with his years of experience in working with business executives and his humorous and delightful packaging of his material, he makes learning with Bob a real joy. But most importantly, anyone who comes in contact with his material is the better for it." **Kim Yost**, CEO Art Van Furniture, former CEO The Brick

Motivate your teams, your employees, and your leaders to 'productively' grow and 'profitably' succeed!

Protect your conference investment - leverage your training dollars.

Enhance your professional career and sell more products and services.

Equip and motivate your leaders and their teams to grow and succeed, 'even' in tough times!

Leverage your time to enhance your skills, equip your teams, and better serve your clients.

Leverage your leadership and investment of time to leave a significant legacy! **Call today** to engage best-selling author, award winning, inspirational leadership keynote speaker, leaders' success coach, and employee development trainer, **Bob 'Idea Man' Hooey** and his innovative, audience based, results-focused, **Ideas At Work!** for your next company, convention, leadership, staff, training, or association event.

You'll be glad you did!

1-780-736-0009 to connect with Bob 'Idea Man' Hooey today

Found this adv many years ago in an old copy of The Saturday Evening Post. It still hangs on my wall by my 'Think Tank' (downstairs hot tub) as an inspiration to continue my creative leadership and to take risks in my life.

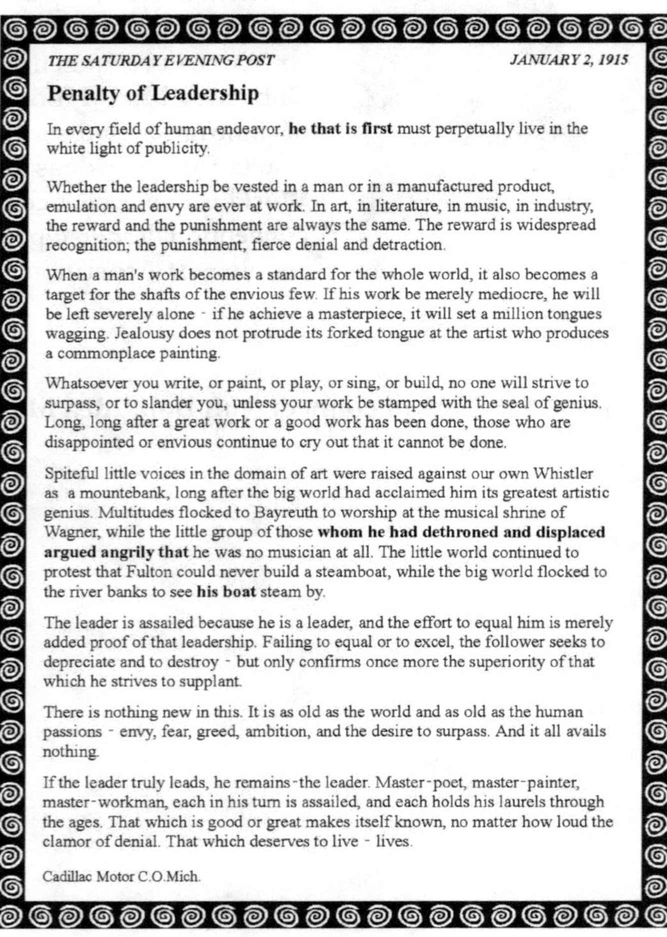

THE SATURDAY EVENING POST *JANUARY 2, 1915*

Penalty of Leadership

In every field of human endeavor, **he that is first** must perpetually live in the white light of publicity.

Whether the leadership be vested in a man or in a manufactured product, emulation and envy are ever at work. In art, in literature, in music, in industry, the reward and the punishment are always the same. The reward is widespread recognition; the punishment, fierce denial and detraction.

When a man's work becomes a standard for the whole world, it also becomes a target for the shafts of the envious few. If his work be merely mediocre, he will be left severely alone - if he achieve a masterpiece, it will set a million tongues wagging. Jealousy does not protrude its forked tongue at the artist who produces a commonplace painting.

Whatsoever you write, or paint, or play, or sing, or build, no one will strive to surpass, or to slander you, unless your work be stamped with the seal of genius. Long, long after a great work or a good work has been done, those who are disappointed or envious continue to cry out that it cannot be done.

Spiteful little voices in the domain of art were raised against our own Whistler as a mountebank, long after the big world had acclaimed him its greatest artistic genius. Multitudes flocked to Bayreuth to worship at the musical shrine of Wagner, while the little group of those **whom he had dethroned and displaced argued angrily that** he was no musician at all. The little world continued to protest that Fulton could never build a steamboat, while the big world flocked to the river banks to see **his boat** steam by.

The leader is assailed because he is a leader, and the effort to equal him is merely added proof of that leadership. Failing to equal or to excel, the follower seeks to depreciate and to destroy - but only confirms once more the superiority of that which he strives to supplant.

There is nothing new in this. It is as old as the world and as old as the human passions - envy, fear, greed, ambition, and the desire to surpass. And it all avails nothing.

If the leader truly leads, he remains - the leader. Master-poet, master-painter, master-workman, each in his turn is assailed, and each holds his laurels through the ages. That which is good or great makes itself known, no matter how loud the clamor of denial. That which deserves to live - lives.

Cadillac Motor C.O.Mich.

www.ingramcontent.com/pod-product-compliance
Lightning Source LLC
Chambersburg PA
CBHW061050220326
41597CB00018BA/2734
9781998014132